BREAKTHROUGH:

THE COMPANION
JOURNAL

FR. ROB GALEA

AVE MARIA PRESS AVE Notre Dame, Indiana

Excerpts from *Breakthrough* copyright © 2018 by Rob Galea. Published by Ave Maria Press, Inc.

Initial concept and compilation by Danielle Sullivan. North American edition compiled by Amber Elder.

Founded in 1865, Ave Maria Press is a ministry of the United States Province of Holy Cross.

www.avemariapress.com

Paperback: ISBN-13 978-1-59471-744-4

Cover and text design by Samantha Watson.

Printed and bound in the United States of America.

How to Use This Journal

This journal is designed to be used with *Breakthrough* by Fr. Rob Galea to help you dive deeper into your relationship with Jesus Christ. It might be your first time reading *Breakthrough* or your third, but this journal is designed to help you reflect on each chapter as you read through the book. The journal's chapters align with *Breakthrough*'s chapters and have questions to help you reflect on your own life and faith journey as you go through the book. All verses come from the NIV translation of the Bible, and you should look up Bible verses referenced in this journal in that translation.

THERE IS NO RIGHT OR WRONG WAY FOR YOU TO USE THIS JOURNAL! IF IT HELPS YOU DEEPEN YOUR RELATIONSHIP WITH JESUS THEN YOU'RE USING IT THE BEST WAY YOU CAN.

1. SURRENDER

GOD LOVES YOU MORE THAN YOU COULD EVER KNOW. HE KNOWS YOUR JOY AND FULLY UNDERSTANDS YOUR PAIN. GOD IS ABLE TO TAKE THAT DARKNESS IN YOUR LIFE, THAT MESS, AND TURN IT INTO A BEAUTIFUL MESSAGE, BUT HE CAN ONLY DO THAT WHEN WE HAND ALL THINGS OVER TO HIM, WHEN WE SURRENDER OUR HEARTS, LIVES, BURDENS, AND PAIN. GOD CREATED YOU FOR JOY, FREEDOM, AND LIFE. HE SAYS IN JOHN 10:10, "I HAVE COME THAT THEY MAY HAVE LIFE, AND HAVE IT TO THE FULL."

(Breakthrough, p. 26)

YOUR

WHAT MOMENTS STAND OUT FROM YOUR PAST THAT HELPED SHAPE WHO YOU ARE TODAY?

WHAT ARE YOU GRATEFUL FOR FROM YOUR PAST?

PAST

HOW WOULD YOU DESCRIBE YOUR RELATIONSHIP WITH JESUS TODAY?

WHAT KIND OF RELATIONSHIP DO YOU DESIRE TO HAVE WITH JESUS?

SURRENDER

WHAT ARE THE EASIEST PARTS OF YOUR LIFE TO SURRENDER TO GOD?

WHAT ARE THE HARDEST PARTS OF YOUR LIFE TO HAND OVER TO GOD?

HERE ARE A FEW SIMPLE THINGS YOU CAN DO TO GROW IN YOUR RELATIONSHIP WITH GOD. HOW CAN YOU SPEND MORE TIME DOING THESE THINGS?

1. **TALKING** TO GOD

2. READING YOUR **BIBLE**

3. PARTICIPATING IN THE **SACRAMENTS**

4. BEING INVOLVED IN A **COMMUNITY** OF FAITH

LORD JESUS, I COME BEFORE YOU, JUST AS I AM. **I AM SORRY** FOR MY SINS; I REPENT OF MY SINS; **PLEASE FORGIVE ME.** IN YOUR NAME, I FORGIVE ALL OTHERS FOR WHAT THEY HAVE DONE AGAINST ME. **I SURRENDER** MY PAIN, ANGER, LONELINESS, SHAME, AND BROKENNESS. YOU KNOW THE DARK, COLD PLACES IN MY HEART; HERE THEY ARE, LORD. TAKE THEM FROM ME. **HELP ME** CARRY THE CROSS THAT I SOMETIMES FIND UNBEARABLE. I GIVE YOU MY ENTIRE SELF, LORD JESUS, AND ASK THAT YOU LET ME KNOW YOU PERSONALLY AND LOVE YOU SELFLESSLY. **HEAL ME, CHANGE ME, AND STRENGTHEN ME** IN BODY, SOUL, AND SPIRIT.

COME, LORD JESUS; COVER ME WITH YOUR PRECIOUS BLOOD, AND **FILL ME WITH YOUR HOLY SPIRIT.** I THANK YOU, JESUS, AND I SHALL FOLLOW YOU EVERY DAY OF MY LIFE. **AMEN.**

MARY, MY MOTHER, QUEEN OF PEACE, ALL THE ANGELS AND SAINTS, **PLEASE HELP ME. AMEN.**

(Breakthrough, p. 26)

"PRESS ON TOWARD THE GOAL TO WIN THE PRIZE FOR WHICH GOD HAS CALLED YOU HEAVENWARD IN CHRIST JESUS."

(Philippians 3:14)

2. PART OF THE GROUP

SLOWLY, IT BEGAN TO DAWN ON ME THAT ALTHOUGH MY RELATIONSHIP WITH GOD WAS PARAMOUNT, I ALSO NEEDED THE LOVING SUPPORT OF A CHRISTIAN COMMUNITY TO ENCOURAGE ME AND WALK WITH ME ON MY JOURNEY. I HOPED THAT THEY NEEDED ME TOO, AS TOGETHER WE BUILT UP THE BODY OF CHRIST.

ST. PAUL, IN HIS LETTER TO THE CORINTHIANS, DESCRIBES THE CHURCH AS THE BODY OF CHRIST. YOU AND I, HE SAYS, ARE PARTICULAR PARTS OF THAT BODY. SOME ARE THE HANDS, OTHERS THE FEET. SOME ARE THE EYES AND OTHERS THE EARS. WE ALL NEED EACH OTHER TO FUNCTION PROPERLY, AND TOGETHER WE ARE ALL DEPENDENT ON CHRIST, THE HEAD OF THE BODY. THE EYE CANNOT SAY TO THE HAND, "I DON'T NEED YOU!" AND THE HEAD CANNOT SAY TO THE FEET, "I DON'T NEED YOU!" (SEE 1 CORINTHIANS 12:12–27).

(*Breakthrough*, p. 38)

COMPANIONS

WHO ARE YOUR SPIRITUAL COMPANIONS, AND HOW ARE YOU JOURNEYING WITH THEM TO SAINTHOOD?

ARE THERE ANY GROUPS YOU BELONG TO THAT ARE HELPING YOU GROW IN FAITH?

WHAT ARE THINGS YOU NEVER COMPROMISE ON? HOW DO YOUR SPIRITUAL COMPANIONS HOLD YOU ACCOUNTABLE TO THEM?

1.

2.

3.

4.

WHAT GIFTS
HAS GOD
GIVEN YOU
THAT YOU
CAN USE TO
GLORIFY HIM?

God's Plan

DO YOU KNOW WHERE OR HOW GOD MIGHT BE CALLING YOU TO SERVE HIM?

HOW DO YOU WANT TO SERVE HIM?

"My hunger for God was growing all the time. I sought God as much as I could. I would take refuge in my room where I would pray, sing songs of praise, pour out my heart to God, and then sit and listen and wait for him to fill my heart. I was totally immersed in the loving presence of God. When I finished my quiet time, I would sit and journal, writing about his involvement in my day and in my prayers. Some days I would write letters to God and then be still and listen to God writing back to me."

(*Breakthrough*, p.33)

HOW HAS GOD BEEN INVOLVED IN YOUR DAY?

IN YOUR PRAYERS?

WHAT IS HE TRYING TO TEACH YOU TODAY?

YOUR LETTER TO GOD

After you pray today, take some time to write your own letter to God.

VISION

WHERE DO YOU WANT TO BE?

WHAT DO YOU WANT TO ACHIEVE?

WHAT GOALS WILL HELP YOU ACHIEVE YOUR VISION?

1.

2.

3.

4.

5.

WHAT ARE YOU PRAYING FOR?

HOW HAVE YOUR SPIRITUAL COMPANIONS RESPONDED TO YOUR GOALS?

Sometimes the vision is vague: "I know I want to serve God and the community" or "I know I want to get out of this pattern of behavior." At other times it is a clearer, long-term picture. Set your goals and remind yourself daily of what you want to achieve.

Persist in Prayer

READ AND REFLECT ON THE FOLLOWING VERSES ABOUT PRAYER. WHAT IS EACH VERSE TEACHING YOU ABOUT PRAYER?

- **1 THESSALONIANS 5:17**

- **EPHESIANS 6:18**

- **ACTS 1:14**

- **JOHN 17:1**

- **LUKE 11:1**

- **PSALM 39:12**

3. RUN TO JESUS

THE WHOLE EXPERIENCE OF "WILL I/WON'T I" WAS A LITTLE LIKE SKYDIVING. . . . YOU MUSTER UP THE COURAGE TO JUMP, AND ONCE YOU DO, YOU FORGET ALL THE FEAR, ALL THE ANXIETY, AND EXPERIENCE NOTHING BUT PURE FREEDOM AND EXHILARATION.

SO MANY MEN AND WOMEN HAVE HEARD GOD'S CALL OVER THEIR LIVES BUT ARE SIMPLY AFRAID TO JUMP. THEY HOLD ON TO THE SIDE OF THE PLANE SO THEY CAN KEEP THEIR OPTIONS OPEN, BUT THE REALITY, AS MENTIONED EARLIER, IS THAT WILL FIND MORE FREEDOM IN ONE COMMITMENT THAN IN HAVING A THOUSAND OPTIONS. THERE IS NOTHING MORE BEAUTIFUL AND FULFILLING THAN RESPONDING TO THE CALL OF GOD.

(*Breakthrough*, p. 66)

FIRST LOVE

HOW CAN YOU KEEP YOUR HEART FOCUSED ON JESUS, OUR FIRST LOVE? (THIS CAN INCLUDE ACTS SUCH AS "PRAYER" AND "ATTENDING MASS" AND ALSO LESS OBVIOUS THINGS SUCH AS "SPENDING TIME IN NATURE" AND "PRACTICING MY GIFTS.")

VOCATION

HAVE YOU CONSIDERED THE DIFFERENT VOCATIONS IN LIFE? IMAGINE YOURSELF LIVING A RELIGIOUS, MARRIED, OR SINGLE LIFE.

WHICH VOCATION DO YOU FEEL CALLED TO BY GOD?

REMEMBER, WHEN YOU FOLLOW GOD'S WILL, YOU OFTEN HAVE A CHOICE BETWEEN GOOD AND BEST, NOT BETWEEN GOOD AND BAD. HAVE YOU EVER HAD TO CHOOSE BETWEEN GOOD AND BEST BEFORE? HOW DID YOU DECIDE?

DISCOVERING GOD'S WILL BY LISTENING TO THE CHURCH

WHEN IT COMES TO DISCOVERING YOUR VOCATION AND LIVING YOUR LIFE, HOW ARE YOU LISTENING TO THE CHURCH? TO YOUR PRIEST? TO CHURCH MEMBERS? TO CHRISTIAN FRIENDS AND FAMILY MEMBERS? TO THE SAINTS?

DEATH TO SELF

WHAT ARE SMALL WAYS YOU CAN PUT OTHERS
FIRST IN YOUR EVERYDAY LIFE?

ARE THERE CHANGES IN YOUR LIFE THAT YOU'RE
PUTTING OFF BECAUSE YOU'RE SCARED?

"GREATER LOVE HAS NO ONE THAN
THIS: TO LAY DOWN ONE'S LIFE FOR
ONE'S FRIENDS." (JOHN 15:13)

"THEN JESUS SAID TO HIS DISCIPLES, 'WHOEVER WANTS TO BE MY DISCIPLE MUST DENY THEMSELVES AND TAKE UP THEIR CROSS AND FOLLOW ME.'" (MATTHEW 16:24)

WHAT DOES CARRYING YOUR CROSS LOOK LIKE FOR YOU?

HOW CAN YOU HELP OTHERS CARRY THEIR CROSSES?

Prayer

SPEAK TO GOD AND ASK HIM WHAT HE WANTS FROM YOUR LIFE. THEN LISTEN TO HIM AS HE SPEAKS TO YOUR HEART. WRITE DOWN WHAT YOU HEAR HIM SAYING TO YOU.

"FOR I KNOW THE PLANS I HAVE FOR YOU, DECLARES THE LORD, PLANS TO PROSPER YOU AND NOT TO HARM YOU, PLANS TO GIVE YOU HOPE AND A FUTURE."

(Jeremiah 29:11)

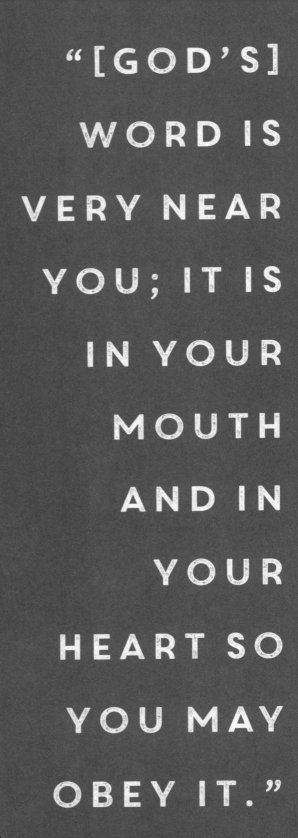

"[GOD'S] WORD IS VERY NEAR YOU; IT IS IN YOUR MOUTH AND IN YOUR HEART SO YOU MAY OBEY IT."

(Deuteronomy 30:14)

4. AT THE FOOT OF THE CROSS

ONE OF MY FAVORITE CHAPTERS IN THE BIBLE IS PSALM 46. VERSE 10 SAYS, "BE STILL AND KNOW THAT I AM GOD." THIS QUOTE, WRITTEN IN MALTESE, WAS PAINTED ABOVE THE TABERNACLE IN THE SEMINARY CHAPEL NEXT TO MY ROOM: *ISKOT! KUNU AFU LI JIEN ALLA.* IT ENCOURAGES THOSE WHO ENTER TO DO SO IN SILENCE.

IT MEANS A LOT MORE TO THE MALTESE READER THAN ANYONE READING IT IN ENGLISH. THE OLD TESTAMENT, INCLUDING THE BOOK OF PSALMS, WAS WRITTEN IN HEBREW, A SEMITIC LANGUAGE. MALTESE IS ALSO A SEMITIC LANGUAGE. THE WORD *ISKOT*, OR "BE STILL," LITERALLY MEANS "SHUT UP." I COULD BE CAUGHT IN THE MIDDLE OF LIFE'S DISTRACTIONS, BUT EVERY TIME I WALKED INTO THE CHAPEL I WAS REMINDED BY GOD TO SHUT UP AND LET HIM TAKE CONTROL.

(*Breakthrough*, p. 87)

HOW MIGHT YOU CHANGE THIS TO MAKE SURE YOU'RE GIVING GOD THE MOST OF YOUR FIRST-FRUITS?

"HONOR THE LORD WITH YOUR WEALTH, WITH THE FIRST-FRUITS OF ALL YOUR INCREASE."
(PROVERBS 3:9)

WRITE DOWN ALL YOUR DREAMS OF THINGS YOU'D LIKE TO DO IN YOUR LIFE.

PSALM 46

GOD IS OUR REFUGE AND OUR STRENGTH,
    an ever-present help in trouble.
Therefore we will not fear, though the earth give way
    and the mountains fall into the heart of the sea,
Though its waters roar and foam
    and the mountains quake with their surging.

There is a river whose streams make glad the city of
      God,
    the holy place where the Most High dwells.
God is within her; she will not fall;
    God will help her at the break of day.
Nations are in uproar; kingdoms fall;
    he lifts his voice, the earth melts.

THE LORD ALMIGHTY IS WITH US;
    THE GOD OF JACOB IS OUR FORTRESS.

Come and see what the LORD has done,
    the desolations he has brought on the earth;
He makes wars cease
    to the ends of the earth.
He breaks the bow and shatters the spear;
    he burns the shields with fire.
HE SAYS, "BE STILL, AND KNOW THAT I
    AM GOD;
    I will be exalted among the nations,
    I will be exalted in the earth."

The LORD Almighty is with us;
    the God of Jacob is our fortress.

A.C.T.S.S.S.

Today, try using this A.C.T.S.S.S. method as you pray. You can journal during each step or you can journal about each step and what you experienced when you are done praying.

ADORATION

Three minutes adoring God for who he is.

. . . .

CONFESSION

Three minutes confessing your sins and your need for him to walk with you every moment.

. . . .

THANKSGIVING

Three minutes thanking God for what he has done in your life and the lives of others.

. . . .

SUPPLICATION

Three minutes praying for the needs of others.

. . . .

SILENCE

Three minutes in absolute silence listening to God speak to your heart.

. . . .

SCRIPTURE

Three minutes reading a passage from the Bible.

. . . .

HOW TO PRAY THE DIVINE MERCY CHAPLET

You can pray the Divine Mercy Chaplet using your ordinary rosary beads. The colored boxes below correspond to the rosary in the illustration above, showing how you can use your rosary to pray each step of the Chaplet.

MAKE THE SIGN OF THE CROSS

In the name of the Father, and of the Son, and of the Holy Spirit. Amen.

OPENING PRAYERS

You expired, Jesus, but the source of life gushed forth for souls, and the ocean of mercy opened up for the whole world. O Fount of Life, unfathomable Divine Mercy, envelop the whole world and empty yourself out upon us.

Repeat three times: O Blood and Water, which gushed forth from the heart of Jesus as a fountain of mercy for us, I trust in you!

PRAY THE OUR FATHER

Our Father, who art in heaven, hallowed be thy name; thy kingdom come; thy will be done on earth as it is in heaven. Give us this day our daily bread; and forgive us our trespasses as we forgave those who trespass against us; and lead us not into temptation, but deliver us from evil. Amen.

PRAY THE HAIL MARY

Hail Mary, full of grace. The Lord is with thee. Blessed art thou amongst women, and blessed is the fruit of thy womb, Jesus. Holy Mary, mother of God, pray for us sinners, now and at the hour of our death. Amen.

PRAY THE APOSTLE'S CREED

I believe in God, the Father almighty, Creator of heaven and earth, and in Jesus Christ, his only Son, our Lord, who was conceived by the Holy Spirit, born of the Virgin Mary, suffered under Pontius Pilate, was crucified, died and was buried; he descended into hell; on the third day he rose again from the dead; he ascended into heaven, and is seated at the right hand of God the Father almighty; from there he will come to judge the living and the dead. I believe in the Holy Spirit, the holy catholic Church, the communion of saints, the forgiveness of sins, the resurrection of the body, and life everlasting. Amen.

PRAY THE ETERNAL FATHER

Eternal Father, I offer you the Body and Blood, Soul and Divinity of your Dearly Beloved Son, our Lord, Jesus Christ, in atonement for our sins and those of the whole world.

ON THE TEN SMALL BEADS OF EACH DECADE

For the sake of his sorrowful Passion, have mercy on us and on the whole world.

PRAY THE ETERNAL FATHER ON THE LARGER BEAD.

Repeat the previous two steps for the remaining decades.

CONCLUSION AND CLOSING PRAYER

Holy God, Holy Mighty One, Holy Immortal One, have mercy on us and on the whole world.

Repeat three times: Eternal God, in whom mercy is endless and the treasury of compassion inexhaustible, look kindly upon us and increase your mercy in us, that in difficult moments we might not despair nor become despondent, but with great confidence submit ourselves to your holy will, which is love and mercy itself.

WHAT IS GOD INSTILLING IN YOUR HEART?

BE PATIENT WITH YOURSELF. YOU WILL OCCASIONALLY LOSE THE HEARTBEAT OF GOD AND FIND IT HARD TO MAINTAIN FOCUS AT TIMES. THERE WILL BE MOMENTS OF LONELINESS AND TIMES WHEN YOU FEEL OVERCOME BY THE DISTRACTIONS OF LIFE, BUT KNOW THAT THERE IS MERCY WAITING FOR YOU EVERY TIME YOU TURN BACK TO GOD.

(Breakthrough, p. 99)

5. PASTORAL ADVENTURES

I WANT TO BE JUST LIKE THE LITTLE BOY WHO SAW A WHOLE BEACH FULL OF WASHED UP STARFISH, AND STARTED THROWING THEM BACK INTO THE OCEAN ONE BY ONE. HE WAS ASKED BY A CURIOUS PASSER-BY WHY HE WAS DOING THAT.

"WHAT DIFFERENCE IS IT GOING TO MAKE?" ASKED THE PASSERBY. "THERE ARE MILLIONS OF STARFISH ON THE BEACH."

THE BOY HELD UP A STARFISH AND SAID, "TO THIS ONE, IT WILL MAKE A DIFFERENCE," AND THEN THREW IT IN THE OCEAN.

I CAN TELL YOU THAT TRYING TO REACH ONE SOUL AT A TIME IS TIRING, HEARTBREAKING, AND OFTEN FEELS FUTILE; BUT I SEE RESULTS, AND THAT IS WHAT KEEPS ME GOING.

(*Breakthrough*, pp. 112–113)

IF YOU'VE EVER LOST A FRIEND, FAMILY MEMBER, OR MENTOR DUE TO DEATH, DISTANCE, OR A FALLING OUT, WHERE DID YOU SEE GOD IN THAT PAIN?

WHAT ARE SOME OF THE WAYS YOU LOOK AFTER YOURSELF WHEN YOU'RE STRUGGLING WITH STRESS OR NEGATIVE EMOTIONS?

HOW DO YOU KEEP YOUR FAITH IN A SECULAR CULTURE? HOW DO YOU KEEP YOUR FAITH WHEN CHRISTIANS DON'T ACT LIKE CHRIST?

THESE THINGS MAKE ME HAPPY:

-
-
-
-
-

HERE'S HOW THEY HELP GROW MY FAITH:

-
-
-
-
-

"DO YOU NOT KNOW THAT YOUR BODIES ARE TEMPLES OF THE HOLY SPIRIT, WHO IS IN YOU, WHOM YOU HAVE RECEIVED FROM GOD? YOU ARE NOT YOUR OWN."

(1 Corinthians 6:19)

PSALM 23

The LORD is my shepherd, I lack nothing
    He makes me lie down in green pastures,
he leads me beside quiet waters,
    he refreshes my soul.
He guides me along the right paths
    for his name's sake
Even though I walk
    through the darkest valley,
I will fear no evil,
    for you are with me;
your rod and your staff,
    they comfort me.

You prepare a table before me
    in the presence of my enemies.
You anoint my head with oil;
    my cup overflows.
Surely your goodness and love will follow me
    all the days of my life,
and I will dwell in the house of the LORD
    forever.

"INVEST YOUR TIME AND ENERGY IN LOVING PEOPLE AND GOD. IN DUE TIME, HE WILL SHOW YOU WHAT YOU ARE TO DO."
—BISHOP JOE GRECH

· ·

DO YOU HAVE SOMEONE WHO HAS TAKEN YOU UNDER THEIR WING AND LOOKED AFTER YOU WHEN YOU WERE STRUGGLING?

IS THERE SOMEONE YOU CAN TAKE UNDER YOUR WING AND LOOK AFTER?

· ·

WE KNOW THAT GOD IS STRONG ENOUGH TO CARRY OUR BURDEN.

"For my yoke is easy and my burden is light."

(Matthew 11:30)

WE CAN SURRENDER OUR HURT TO GOD BECAUSE HE CARES FOR US.

"Cast all your anxiety on him because he cares for you."

(1 Peter 5:7)

WE CAN REST IN THE HOLY SPIRIT.

"And I will ask the Father, and he will give you another advocate to help you and be with you forever."

(John 14:16)

IN THE STORM OF GRIEF AND PAIN, GOD CAN BE OUR ANCHOR. WE CAN RELY ON THE COMMUNITY OF THE CHURCH, DIG DEEP INTO THE TRUTH OF THE WORD, AND FIND HOPE KNOWING THAT EVEN HERE, GOD HAS NOT LEFT OUR SIDE.

"We have this hope as an anchor for the soul, firm and secure. It enters the inner sanctuary behind the curtain, where our forerunner, Jesus, has entered on our behalf. He has become a high priest forever, in the order of Melchizedek."

(Hebrews 6:19–20)

TRUST

WRITE TO JESUS ASKING HIM TO LEAD
YOU AND HELP YOU TRUST HIM NO
MATTER WHERE HE LEADS.

6. RECEIVE THE POWER

I DID NOT WAIT FOR GOD TO GIVE ME COURAGE BUT REPEATEDLY STEPPED FORWARD IN MY FEAR AND DISAPPOINTMENT. I FAILED OVER AND OVER AGAIN, AND FOR A WHILE IT SEEMED THAT WITH EVERY FOOT I PUT FORWARD, I TOOK TEN STEPS BACK. . . . I DID NOT WANT TO MISS OUT ON THIS GOD-GIVEN DREAM WHILE WAITING FOR GOD TO TAKE AWAY MY FEAR. I WAS FEARFUL, I WAS SCARED, BUT I DID IT IN SPITE OF MY FEAR—I DID IT SCARED.

(*Breakthrough*, pp. 142–143)

ARE YOU AN INTROVERT OR EXTROVERT? HOW DOES THIS AFFECT HOW YOU FOLLOW GOD?

WHAT WOULD YOU DO IF YOU KNEW YOU COULD NOT FAIL?

· ·

"THE ONE WHO CALLS YOU IS
FAITHFUL, AND HE WILL DO IT."
(1 THESSALONIANS 5:24)

WHAT ARE YOUR TOP THREE PRIORITIES?

1.

2.

3.

"WE ARE ALL CALLED TO BE EVANGELISTS, TO SPREAD THE GOOD NEWS TO THOSE AROUND US. PEOPLE ARE DESPERATE FOR THE TRUTH OF GOD'S UNCONDITIONAL LOVE AND PROMISE OF SALVATION. THIS FREEDOM IS THEIRS, BUT THEY NEED TO KNOW WHERE TO RECEIVE IT."

(*Breakthrough*, p. 152)

HOW CAN YOU SHARE THE GOOD NEWS WITH THE PEOPLE AROUND YOU?

"SURROUND YOURSELF WITH PEOPLE WHO WILL REMIND YOU THAT IT NEVER WAS AND NEVER SHOULD BE ABOUT YOU BUT ONLY TO GIVE GOD THE GLORY."
(Breakthrough, p. 154)

HOW CAN YOU LIVE YOUR LIFE AND PURSUE YOUR DREAMS IN A WAY THAT GIVES GOD THE GLORY?

HAVE OBSTACLES EVER PREVENTED YOU FROM PURSUING YOUR DREAMS? HOW HAVE YOU OVERCOME THEM? HOW CAN YOU TRY TO OVERCOME THEM?

WHAT DREAMS THAT YOU WROTE DOWN IN CHAPTER 4 DO YOU HAVE FOR YOUR LIFE? ARE THESE DREAMS GOD HAS PLACED ON YOUR HEART?

HOW CAN YOU PRIORITIZE YOUR GOD-GIVEN DREAMS OVER OTHER DREAMS YOU HAVE FOR YOUR LIFE?

"A GOD-GIVEN DREAM INVOLVES ABOUT FULFILLING GOD'

WHAT PRICE ARE YOU WILLING TO PAY FOR GOD TO FULFILL THE DREAMS PLACED IN YOUR HEART?

WHAT DO YOU HAVE TO DO TO WORK WITH GOD TO REALIZE THESE DREAMS?

BUT IS NEVER ABOUT US. IT IS ALL
URPOSE IN THIS WORLD."

(Breakthrough, p. 154)

DO IT SCARED.

"NOW FAITH IS CONFIDENCE IN WHAT WE HOPE FOR AND ASSURANCE ABOUT WHAT WE DO NOT SEE."

(Hebrews 11:1)

7. THE X FACTOR

THE CHURCH, THAT IS, YOU AND I, NEEDS TO GO WHERE PEOPLE ARE. WE NEED TO UNDERSTAND THAT THE FIRST THING THAT PEOPLE WILL CONNECT WITH, BOTH YOUNG AND OLD, MAY NOT BE THE TRANSCENDENCE OF GOD BUT THE HUMANITY OF THE PERSON COMMUNICATING THE MESSAGE. THE CHURCH NEEDS TO BECOME A ROLE MODEL. WE KNOW THE REASONS WHY IT HAS LOST ITS CREDIBILITY AS A ROLE MODEL AND THAT IS WHY THE NEXT GENERATION—OUR GENERATION—NEEDS TO RISE UP AND CREATE A NEW GENERATION OF ROLE MODELS WHOM PEOPLE WANT TO BE LIKE: REAL, HUMAN ROLE MODELS WHO ARE COMMITTED TO JESUS.

(Breakthrough, p. 161)

"THIS IS THE POWER OF MUSIC. IT CAN TRANSCEND THOUGHTS, IDEOLOGIES, CULTURES, LANGUAGES, AND RELIGION."
(Breakthrough, 158)

WHAT ARE SOME OF YOUR FAVORITE LYRICS?
HOW ARE THEY HELPING DRAW YOU CLOSER TO GOD?

HOW CAN YOU BE A TRUE REFLECTION OF CHRIST—NOT JUST IN WORDS AND ACTIONS BUT IN ALL THAT YOU ARE?

"TO SHARE THE GOSPEL IS NOT ONLY ABOUT THE WORDS WE SPEAK OR THE WAY WE ACT. TRUE EVANGELIZATION IS BECOMING A PERFECT ICON OR REFLECTION OF JESUS. IN ORDER TO BE A PERFECT REFLECTION, IT MEANS WE HAVE TO HIDE, TO GET OUT OF THE WAY OF THE MIRROR."

(*Breakthrough*, p. 159)

"YOU NEED TO **COMMIT** TO **DAILY PRAYER**, TO THE **SACRAMENTS**, AND TO HAVE **OTHER FAITHFUL** PEOPLE AROUND YOU WHO CAN SPEAK INTO YOUR HEART WHEN YOU YOURSELF GET TO CLOSE TO THE CLIFF EDGE. **AT THE EDGE, THE STRUGGLE AND THE TEMPTATIONS ARE REAL.**"

(*Breakthrough*, p. 163)

WHAT IS YOUR CLIFF EDGE? IS IT ADDICTIONS, DISTRACTIONS, BAD COMPANY, OR SOMETHING ELSE ALTOGETHER?

WHERE CAN YOU STEP OUT IN FAITH **TO HELP OTHERS** FIND JOY AND SALVATION?

PRESENCE

WRITE A LIST OF CATHOLICS WHO INSPIRE YOU.
THEY CAN BE SAINTS, MUSICIANS, PEOPLE IN
YOUR PARISH, PEOPLE YOU FOLLOW ON SOCIAL
MEDIA, AUTHORS, AND ANYONE ELSE WHOSE FAITH
INSPIRES YOU TO LIVE YOURS.

CREDIBILITY OF PRESENCE

WHERE DO YOU SPEND MOST OF
YOUR TIME? IS IT AT HOME, WORK,
THE LOCAL CAFÉ, SCHOOL, COLLEGE?
ARE YOU A WITNESS FOR JESUS
IN THESE PLACES?

"WHAT GOOD WILL IT BE FOR SOMEONE TO GAIN THE WHOLE WORLD, YET FORFEIT THEIR SOUL? OR WHAT CAN ANYONE GIVE IN EXCHANGE FOR THEIR SOUL?"

(Matthew 16:26)

WHAT RESOURCES DO YOU HAVE TO GIVE TO GOD?

IF YOU HAD A CHANCE TO EVANGELIZE, HOW WOULD YOU DO IT?

HOW CAN YOU STEP OUT IN FAITH?

8. GOD'S EYE VIEW

YOU AND I WERE NOT CREATED TO WALK IN THIS WORLD ALONE. HOWEVER, GOD RESPECTS OUR FREE WILL, AND SHOULD WE WANT TO JOURNEY THROUGH LIFE ALONE, HE WILL ALLOW US, BUT EVEN THEN, HE IS NEVER FAR BEHIND. WALKING ALONE, WE CANNOT SEE THE WORLD OR EXPERIENCE FREEDOM AND THE JOY OF THIS LIFE TO EXTENT THAT GOD HAS CREATED US TO. AWAY FROM THIS WE CANNOT LIVE LIFE IN THE ABUNDANCE THAT GOD HAS FOR US (SEE JOHN 10:10). AT THE MOMENT WE ARE READY TO ADMIT THAT WE NEED GOD'S HELP, WE CAN RAISE OUR HANDS IN SURRENDER TO HIM, AND HE WILL RUN TOWARDS US AND LIFT US INTO HIS ARMS. FROM THERE, STRONG AND SECURE, WE WILL BE ABLE TO SEE THE WORLD FROM GOD'S EYES, JUST THE WAY WE WERE CREATED TO SEE IT. EVEN THERE WE MAY GO THROUGH THE VALLEY OF THE SHADOW OF DARKNESS, BUT WALKING IN A RELATIONSHIP WITH GOD AND ATTACHED TO HIS BODY, THE CHURCH, WE WILL NEVER NEED TO FEAR ANY TRIAL OR EVIL BECAUSE HE WILL BE THERE WITH YOU, HOLDING YOU CLOSE AND CARRYING YOU TO HIS EYE VIEW (SEE PSALMS 23:4).

(Breakthrough, p. 179)

HOW DO YOU THINK YOUR VIEW OF YOUR LIFE COMPARES
TO HOW GOD SEES YOUR LIFE?

HOW CAN YOU ALLOW GOD TO MOLD YOU INTO AN
INSTRUMENT TO BUILD UP THE KINGDOM?

"IN A RELATIONSHIP WITH JESUS, EMPOWERED BY HIS HOLY SPIRIT AND SUSTAINED BY HIS BODY, THE CHURCH, LIFE WILL CONTINUE TO HAVE ITS CROSSES, BUT YOU WILL FIND STRENGTH YOU NEVER KNEW YOU HAD TO PICK UP YOUR CROSS AND JOYFULLY FOLLOW HIM. WITH GOD BESIDE YOU, YOU WILL BE ABLE TO SEE AND EXPERIENCE THE WORLD FROM A DIFFERENT AND HIGHER PERSPECTIVE."

(*Breakthrough*, p. 176)

"ALWAYS BE PREPARED TO GIVE AN ANSWER TO ANYONE WHO ASKS YOU TO GIVE THE REASON FOR THE HOPE THAT YOU HAVE."

(1 Peter 3:15)

BE PREPARED

LIST THREE THINGS ABOUT YOUR FAITH YOU WANT TO LEARN MORE ABOUT.

1.

2.

3.

AFTER RESEARCHING, WRITE DOWN WHAT YOU LEARNED ABOUT THOSE THINGS.

1.

2.

3.

"YOU HAVE AS MUCH A CALL AND NEED TO EVANGELIZE AS I DO AND THE POPE DOES."

(Breakthrough, p. 183)

WHO MIGHT LISTEN TO YOU BEFORE THEY LISTEN TO A PRIEST, A NUN, OR THE POPE?

HOW CAN YOU EVANGELIZE TO THOSE PEOPLE TODAY?

TYPES OF LOVE

Agape

This is unconditional love. There is no greater love than this, and the greatest expression of this love is to die for someone (see John 15:13) as Jesus did for you and me.

Philia

This is the love of a mate, brother, or sister. It's a deep friendship. Not nearly as perfect as *agape*, but love nonetheless.

WHEN YOU THINK OF GOD, WHAT KIND OF LOVE DO YOU THINK OF? WHAT KIND OF LOVE DOES HE GIVE YOU? WHAT KIND OF LOVE DO YOU GIVE HIM IN RESPONSE?

"JESUS DOES NOT WAIT FOR YOU TO BE PERFECT AND WITHOUT SIN TO SERVE HIM."

(Breakthrough, p. 181)

> "I DO NOT UNDERSTAND WHAT I DO. FOR WHAT I WANT TO DO, I DO NOT DO, BUT WHAT I HATE I DO."
>
> (Romans 7:15)

DO YOU EVER MESS UP AND DO THINGS THAT YOU KNOW YOU SHOULD NOT DO, THAT YOU DON'T EVEN REALLY WANT TO DO, AND THAT YOU REGRET AFTERWARD? DO YOU EVER MESS UP BY NOT DOING SOMETHING YOU WANT TO DO OR KNOW YOU SHOULD DO? CONSIDER A TIME WHEN YOU'VE FELT LIKE ST. PAUL, AND WRITE DOWN WAYS THAT, WITH GOD'S HELP, YOU COULD BEGIN TO DO MORE OF THE GOOD THINGS AND LESS OF THE BAD.

"Jesus, if you can take this mess and make something out of it, here I am."

WHAT MESS DO YOU HAVE TO OFFER GOD?

GOD'S-EYE VIEW

When in your life have you walked away or turned your back on God? Write a letter to God asking forgiveness for these times.

9. BY THE GRACE OF GOD

STOP MAKING EXCUSES. STOP GIVING IN TO FEAR. GOD WILL NOT CONDEMN YOU. HE WILL NOT REJECT YOU. HE WILL NEVER ABANDON YOU. TRUST GOD AND JUMP OUT OF THE NEST OF FEAR, BELIEVING THAT HE WILL CATCH YOU. GOD HAS A GREAT PURPOSE FOR YOUR LIFE, BUT YOU HAVE A CHOICE: TO STAY IN THE NEST OF COMFORT, FEAR, AND SHAME, OR TO GET UP AND FACE YOUR FEAR AND BECOME ALL THAT GOD CREATED YOU TO BE. GOD WILL BE RIGHT THERE BESIDE YOU, TO PROTECT AND INSPIRE YOU (SEE PSALM 9:18–15).

(Breakthrough, p. 195)

"YOU ARE A CHILD OF GOD AND CAPABLE OF BECOMING LIKE JESUS."

(*Breakthrough*, p. 194)

WHEN HAVE YOU BEEN THRUST OUT OF YOUR COMFORT ZONE? HOW HAVE THOSE MOMENTS HELPED YOU BECOME ALL THAT YOU WERE CREATED TO BE?

HOW CAN YOU BE A

WORLD CHANGER?

HISTORY-MAKER?

CHAMPION?

SAINT?

HOW TO

1. FIND YOUR CENTER OF GRAVITY

**WHAT IS YOUR CENTER OF GRAVITY?
WHAT DO YOU HAVE TO STAND ON WHEN THE
WORLD AROUND YOU SHAKES?**

OVERCOME EXCUSES

2. GET YOUR BUTT TO THE GROUND

HOW CAN YOU TRUST IN GOD'S PLAN, EVEN WHEN YOU FEEL LIKE A FAILURE?

3. GET UP AGAIN

WHAT WILL YOU DO WITH THE STRENGTH THAT CHRIST GIVES YOU?

GOD HAS MANY NAMES IN THE BIBLE: *EL SHADDAI*, *JEHOVAH-RAAH*, *ADONAI*, *EL OLAM*, *BAAL PERAZIM*. LOOK UP DIFFERENT NAMES FOR GOD IN YOUR BIBLE, AND WRITE THEM AND WHAT THEY TELL YOU ABOUT GOD HERE. IS THERE ANY ONE NAME THAT SPEAKS TO YOU THE MOST RIGHT NOW?

BAAL PERAZIM, LORD OF THE BREAKTHROUGH

WHAT WALLS IN YOUR LIFE DOES *BAAL PERAZIM* HAVE TO WORK THROUGH IN YOUR LIFE?

"I CAN DO THIS THROUGH HIM WHO GIVES ME STRENGTH"

(Philippians 4:13)

"GETTING UP AGAIN IS ABOUT UNDERSTANDING THE PURPOSE AND PLAN GOD HAS FOR YOUR LIFE. AS YOU RAISE YOURSELF, YOU MAY NOT HAVE ALL THE ANSWERS, SO IN HUMILITY SURRENDER TO GOD AND LIFT OTHERS WITH YOU AS YOU POINT TO THE ONE WHO HOLDS YOU IN HIS ARMS: JESUS."

(*Breakthrough*, p. 199)

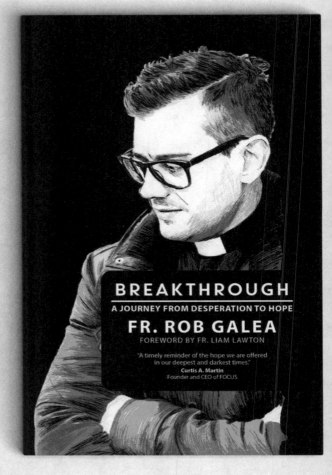